The NASTY past

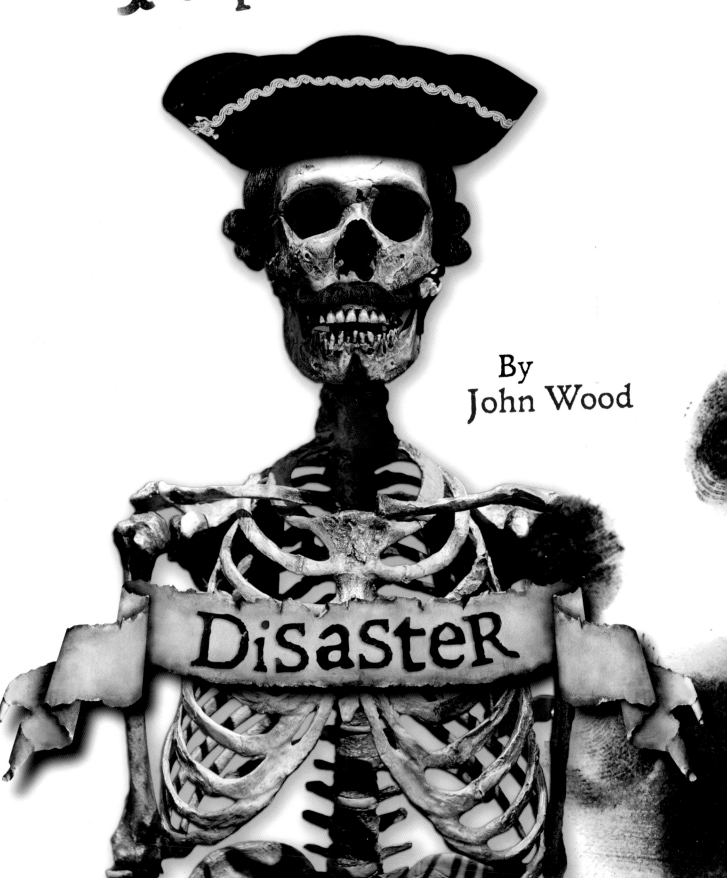

By
John Wood

Disaster

BookLife
PUBLISHING

©2019
BookLife Publishing Ltd.
King's Lynn
Norfolk PE30 4LS

ISBN: 978-1-78637-592-6

Written by:
John Wood

Edited by:
Madeline Tyler

Designed by:
Dan Scase

PHOTO CREDITS

Contents

Words that look like **THIS** are explained in the glossary on page 31.

A Discovery from the Past

There are secrets underground. It's not all dirt and mud, especially if you know where to look. Buried under all that earth and rock are clues to the past. Whether it's bones, bodies, books or weapons, each clue tells a story of something that happened a long time ago. And it turns out that these stories can be pretty gruesome...

The people who find and study old, historical objects are called archaeologists (say: ar–kee–ol–uh–jists).

The past wasn't a nice place to live. People didn't live as long as they do now, and there were plenty of things to kill them before they even reached old age. Towns were dirty, work was brutal, and disease and war were everywhere. Despite all this, people still made pottery and jewellery, built homes and temples, and lived their lives. Some of the things they made are still in the earth with their bones, waiting to be found...

It might not seem like it, but these archaeologists are very, very excited right now.

A NEW STORY

Here in this museum, all sorts of objects are collected so people can learn about history. There are even skeletons of people who died long ago. Look, here is one! This skeleton is covered in some sort of hard powder. The bones look quite old – this person must have died more than a hundred years ago. They were found in Indonesia. What happened to this person all that time ago? Who were they, and how did they die?

The **REMAINS** show that the person probably died in some sort of disaster. But to find out exactly how this person met their end, you must travel through history. Take a note of each disaster you learn about and see if any of them might explain our skeleton here. But be careful – the past can be very, very dangerous.

The Asteroid That Probably Killed the Dinosaurs

Natural disasters can be cruel. They can also be scary. Disasters can wipe entire **SPECIES** off the face of the Earth – it has happened before! Before we get to how dangerous disasters can be for humans, let's have a look at what happened to the dinosaurs.

It doesn't matter how big and scary your teeth are, T. rex, you are still going to die!

SOMETHING FROM SPACE?

Some **SCIENTISTS** think that the dinosaurs died because of a giant rock from space. Around 65 million years ago, an asteroid that was 9 kilometres wide smashed into the planet at the Yucatan Peninsula in Mexico. The dinosaurs would have seen a blinding light in the sky as it burned bigger and brighter than the Sun. Then the meteorite would have slammed into the ground, throwing up lots of dust and **DEBRIS**.

The asteroid struck in shallow seas, causing a huge amount of soot and dust to fill the air. If it had struck almost anywhere else, this might not have happened, and the terrible lizards might still be roaming the world...

SOMETHING DEEPER UNDERGROUND?

Other scientists think that the dinosaurs died because of volcanic eruptions. A huge amount of lava and **ASH** might have been spurting out of supervolcanoes from deep underground. These eruptions would have taken place around 65 million years ago in an area that is now India.

The few remaining dinosaurs left EVOLVED into

END OF THE WORLD?

Whether the disaster was an asteroid or volcanic eruptions, the effects were terrifying. The whole world was forced into a winter that lasted for years. Because of all the dust and debris in the air, very little sunlight could get through. This meant the world got colder. Some historians and scientists believe that no sunlight reached the ground for two years. This was very bad for plants, which need sunlight to stay alive. As plants died, so did the animals that ate plants. Soon, there was very little food left for any living thing.

If there was an asteroid, giant fireballs would have rained down on Earth from the impact.

After the skies finally cleared, there were still **GASES** in the air that would have trapped lots of heat on Earth. This meant that the world suddenly warmed up a lot. Many animals couldn't cope with all these changes. During this time, around three-quarters of the life on Earth was killed, including **NON-AVIAN** dinosaurs. They never stood a chance against disaster.

An asteroid would also have caused tsunamis – huge waves that would have destroyed everything in their path.

The White Ship

On the 25th of November, 1120, Prince William Adelin was getting ready to sail back to England. After fighting lots of Frenchmen and winning important battles in France, he was ready to go home. His dad, King Henry I, had picked out a special ship for William to travel on: the White Ship. However, little did they know that everything was about to go wrong...

FIT FOR A PRINCE

Prince William was the heir to the throne. This meant that when Henry I died, William would become king. Henry I did not have any other sons that could be his heir. Because of this, William was an important man and, like other important men at the time, he had lots of people who followed him around and travelled with him. The White Ship was going to be full of 140 knights, 18 **NOBLEMEN** and many other rich people. William was also joined by his cousins, as well as his half-brother, Richard, and his half-sister, Matilda. At night, they set off for England.

Haven't you knights got something better to do?

BLAME IT ON THE GOOD TIMES

The White Ship left from a harbour called Barfleur. This harbour was known for being dangerous. It had a strong **CURRENT** and lots of rocks. However, William and his crew weren't worried about that – they were too busy partying! Both the passengers and crew aboard the ship became very loud and excited. Some monks came to bless the ship, but they were shouted at and chased off by William's friends. When the ship set sail, the revellers decided to race the King's ship, but struck a rock on the port side...

A COUNTRY IN CHAOS

Around 300 people died, including Prince William Adelin.

Only one person from the ship survived; he was a seventeen-year-old butcher from a town called Rouen. It was his job to tell people the terrible news. But everything was about to get worse for all of England. After King Henry I died, there was no clear heir to the throne. For many years afterwards, people fought over the throne and tried to decide who should run the country. This **PERIOD** was known as The Anarchy.

The captain of the ship, Thomas FitzStephen, was floating along after the ship sank. When he heard that Prince William Adelin had died, he drowned himself instead of facing the King.

When the King heard that his only son had died, it is said that he fell to the ground in sadness and never smiled again.

The Lisbon Earthquake

Many disasters destroy lives and cost lots of money. However, some disasters can change how we think. The Lisbon earthquake was one of these disasters. It all started on the 1st of November, 1755. It was a sunny day. Most people in Lisbon were praying to God in church because it was All Saints' Day, which is an important day for **CHRISTIANS**. Suddenly, everybody heard a deep rumble which became louder and louder. The city began to shake and bells started ringing. Then the city of Lisbon was hit with one of the biggest earthquakes in the history of Europe.

Buildings collapsed, and many people were crushed under the falling debris. The churches fell down too, killing those inside. Suddenly, the city was hit by a huge tsunami that was caused by the earthquake. The tsunami waves also travelled across the seas to other countries; the tsunami caused damage to Spain, Ireland and even some Caribbean islands. And if that wasn't enough, the earthquake also started a big fire in Lisbon.

The waves that hit Lisbon were around six metres high – that is taller than three adults!

Around 12,000 houses were destroyed in Lisbon.

LISBON WANTED ANSWERS

The people of Lisbon were not happy. Many wanted to know why God had sent an earthquake to a very **RELIGIOUS** city full of people praying. It didn't seem fair to punish people when they had done nothing wrong. People wrote books and poems about the earthquake. In these books, they said that religion didn't always make sense.

Nobody can say for sure how many people died all over the world because of this earthquake, although it was probably around 60,000.

Gassy caverns? What were you thinking, Kant?

Soon, some people questioned whether God had even sent the earthquake at all. A man called Immanuel Kant came up with an idea that underground caverns full of hot gases were the cause of the earthquake. Even though this idea was completely wrong, it was one of the first times people had tried to explain disasters using nature, rather than thinking that they came from God. The Lisbon earthquake of 1755 was one of the big events that changed how Europeans thought about God and religion.

The Great Fire of London

On Tuesday the 4th of September, 1666, London was burning. It was one of the worst fires to ever spread through the city. It would take 10 million pounds and 50 years to rebuild the city. And it all started in one building. This is the story of a very unlucky baker.

London had no fire brigade at this time. People fought the fire themselves using leather buckets, axes and water squirts. But it was no use.

Thomas Farriner owned the king's bakery on Pudding Lane. On Saturday night, he filled his oven with coals as he usually did and went to bed. However, on that night, a spark flew out of the oven and started a fire in the bakery. Soon the whole building was on fire, and Thomas Farriner had to escape through an upstairs window with his daughter. Unfortunately for Thomas, and the rest of London, it had been a very hot summer. This meant there had been no rain, and all the wooden buildings were very dry. This made perfect fuel for fire. Strong gusts of wind also helped the fire travel quickly.

When he was woken up and told about the fire, the mayor said that it wasn't that bad, and went back to bed. Silly mayor.

The fire quickly spread through Pudding Lane and then down Fish Hill. Samuel Pepys, who also lived on Pudding Lane, kept a diary of the event. After burying his best cheese and running off to another part of London, he described the panic that everybody felt. Many people ran through the streets, while others tried to escape the fire on boats down the river. To take away the fire's fuel, buildings were pulled down using hooks. However, it was no use – the fire was too quick.

"Lord! What sad sight it was by moonelight to see, the whole City almost on fire, that you might see it plain at Woolwich, as if you were by it." Samuel Pepys

Even the King helped put out the fire.

The fire lasted for several days. By the Tuesday, the flames reached St Paul's Cathedral. The metal roof melted and poured into the street. By the Thursday, the fire was finally out. It had destroyed 13,200 houses and 87 churches. St Paul's Cathedral, 52 **LIVERY HALLS** and the Guildhall (the mayor's office) were also destroyed. Like many disasters, the Great Fire of London came about because of a mixture of things all happening at once – windy weather, a dry summer and one very unlucky baker.

ST PAUL'S CATHEDRAL

The Titanic

On the 10th of April, 1912, the Titanic left England for its first journey; it was going to New York, in the US. At the time, it was the biggest ship in the world, with over 2,000 people on board. The ship had restaurants, a gym, a library and a swimming pool. It even had a live orchestra! All sorts of people were on the ship, from the captain and the crew to some of the richest people in the world. However, none of these people knew that a disaster was going to happen – a disaster that the world would never forget.

The Titanic was known as "The Unsinkable Ship".

SOMEWHERE IN THE ATLANTIC...

On the fifth day of the journey, there were reports of ice in the water. However, the captain, Edward Smith, carried on at high speeds. That night, there was no moonlight, and the waters were completely still. The ocean was freezing cold and dangerous. Suddenly, the lookout telephoned the captain, shouting "Iceberg, right ahead!". Captain Smith tried to turn the ship, but it was too late.

This is believed to be the iceberg that sank the Titanic. The iceberg was spotted by another crew the next day with a "red smear" of paint, indicating it had hit a ship.

In the end, more than 1,500 people died.

The Titanic hit the iceberg hard, and there was a lot of damage. The ship began to fill with water. However, because it was so big, the Titanic took over two hours to sink. At first, the passengers didn't panic because they thought they were safe. However, soon one end of the ship began to rise out of the water, as the other sank into the sea. It was a disaster. There were not enough lifeboats to carry people away, and those who were left on the ship gathered on the end that was stuck up in the air. Some of them jumped off into the ocean, while others waited for the whole thing to slowly disappear into the dark water.

STORIES FROM THE TITANIC

The Titanic now lies at the bottom of the Atlantic Ocean.

As the ship sank, an Englishman called William T. Stead was seen sitting down, quietly reading. A woman called Ida Straus refused to get on a lifeboat without her husband. A boy called Jack Thyer jumped into the water and swam as hard as he could – and he survived!

Ice Ages

The temperature of the Earth has changed a lot since it was formed around 4.5 billion years ago. For the first few million years, the world was very hot; the air would have been almost 2,000 degrees Celsius (°C) and the surface would have been made from lava. However, the world can go through periods when it is very cold too. These are called ice ages. During an ice age, there can be times when the ice covers even more of the world than usual. This is called glaciation (say: glay-see-ay-shun), and it can be a real disaster for anything that is not well prepared.

SNOW ESCAPE

The last big glaciation ended about 10,000 years ago. Around 18,000 years ago it was at its most powerful; the ice sheets were over 3.6 kilometres thick in some places, and covered what is now South America, Canada, Scandinavia and Russia. During the ice age, there were many giant animals such as woolly mammoths, woolly rhinos and sabre-toothed tigers that could be found wandering the snow.

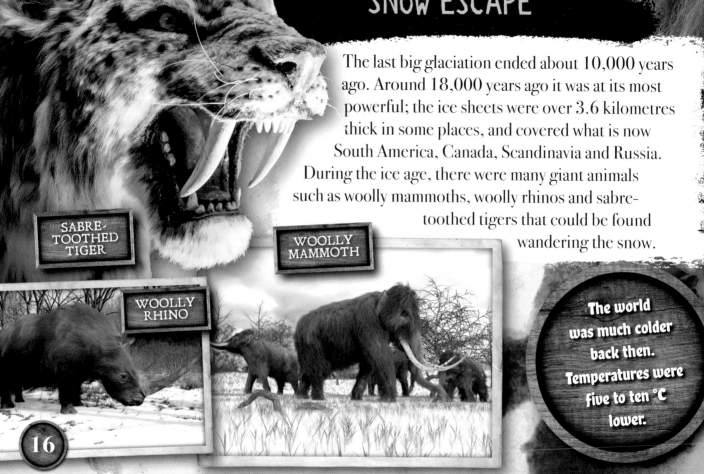

SABRE-TOOTHED TIGER

WOOLLY MAMMOTH

WOOLLY RHINO

The world was much colder back then. Temperatures were five to ten °C lower.

Sea levels were around 121 metres lower during the last glaciation.

Glaciation was difficult for many animals. Humans had to be smart; they made new tools and carefully chose where they lived. During this time, humans used new, icy land bridges to explore **CONTINENTS** where they had never been before. Neanderthals were a species who were very similar to humans. However, they died out around the same time as humans began to become **SUCCESSFUL**. Some historians think this is because humans were better at finding and using **RESOURCES**.

NEANDERTHAL

After the end of this glaciation, many animals found it difficult to deal with the hotter temperatures. Woolly mammoths and sabre-toothed tigers disappeared and died out. Humans, meanwhile, were able to adapt quickly and survive. The ice age shows that what is a disaster for some can be an opportunity for others. When the temperatures rose, so did the humans. It was time for us to go out there and explore the world!

The Yellow River Floods

The Yellow River is a lot more dangerous than it looks here.

One of the deadliest disasters in history happened in China in 1887. After very heavy rain, the second-longest river in China, the Yellow River, flooded. The river flooded very easily, so this wasn't out of the ordinary. However, this time it killed at least 900,000 people and destroyed 11 large towns and hundreds of villages. Some historians think it might even have killed two million people.

When the water overcame the banks, there was destruction everywhere. To escape the flooding, people climbed trees, or clambered to the roofs of their houses. Anyone with a boat sailed down the flooded streets to rescue those in trouble. However, most people had small rowing boats, so rescuing others was slow. It was autumn, and there were strong winds. This made people cold and hungry as they waited for help.

Millions of people were left homeless after the flood.

One family knew there was no way they could survive the flood. They put their baby on top of a wooden chest. Next to the baby they placed food and a piece of paper with the baby's name on it. Then they pushed the chest out on the water, where it floated downstream. Luckily, the chest stayed afloat long enough for the baby to be rescued.

LIVING BY THE RIVER

If rivers in history were so dangerous, why did people live so close to them? Rivers provide food and transport. The soil near a river can be especially good for farming, as **CROPS** grow bigger and faster. Today, we have **TECHNOLOGY** to warn us of disasters, but in the Nasty Past, people had to take bigger risks.

The Year without a Summer

In the middle of June, in 1816, American children put on hats and gloves and grabbed their sleds. Even though it was summer, they were going to play in the snow. At the same time, crops were failing all over the world, from Ireland to China. Disease spread over Europe because people were weak with hunger. The whole world was much colder than usual. 1816 was the year without a summer for the whole world, and it was all because of one giant, gassy explosion.

Like most gassy explosions, this one probably smelt really, really bad.

VIOLENT VOLCANOES

The explosion came from a volcano called Mount Tambora, in Indonesia. It was 1815, and local people heard a rumbling sound from the ground. Suddenly, there was a huge explosion. The sound of the eruption was heard on islands that were 2,600 kilometres away. Then, five days later, it happened again. This explosion was the biggest one ever recorded on Earth. Three columns of fire shot upwards, and a **PLUME** of smoke reached into the sky, over 40 kilometres high.

In one local language, the volcano's name means 'gone' because so many people have disappeared on its slopes.

Many people didn't even know that Mount Tambora was a volcano because it hadn't erupted in so long.

MEANWHILE...

500 metres of the volcano were blown off as it exploded.

Soldiers who were hundreds of kilometres away thought the sound was a cannon, and that they were being attacked. They ran around, trying to find out who was shooting. However, the explosion they heard was far more powerful than any cannon. When volcanoes erupt, they release something called a pyroclastic (say: pie-row-class-tik) flow. This is a deadly flow of gas, ash and blocks of lava. Mount Tambora's pyroclastic flow burst down the slopes at 100 kilometres per hour.

Cannons were the least of the soldiers' worries.

Mount Tambora

CHANGING THE WORLD

The volcano threw a huge amount of ash into the air. For weeks afterwards, the ash rained back down to Earth, covering entire islands with a thick, grey blanket. Mount Tambora also spewed out **PARTICLES** of something called sulphur. These sulphur particles stayed in the air, slowly spreading around the planet. The sulphur created a sort of fog that blocked a lot of sunlight from getting to Earth. And without sunlight, there isn't much of a summer.

The Locust Plague

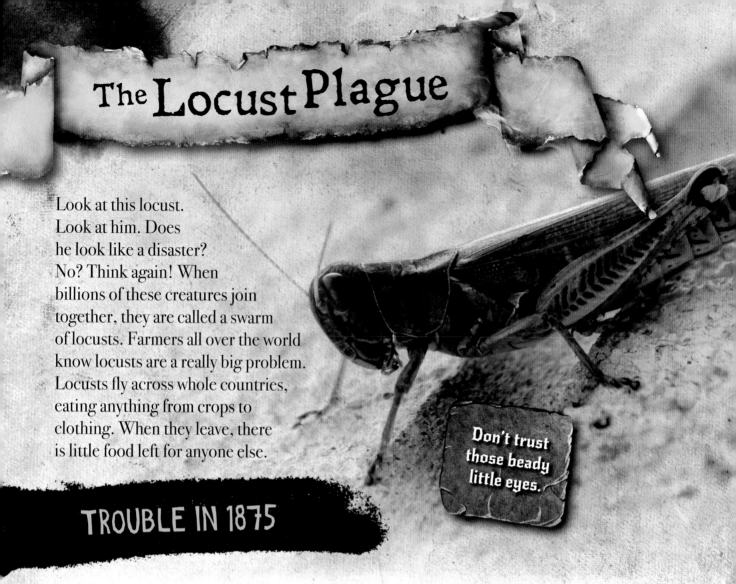

Look at this locust. Look at him. Does he look like a disaster? No? Think again! When billions of these creatures join together, they are called a swarm of locusts. Farmers all over the world know locusts are a really big problem. Locusts fly across whole countries, eating anything from crops to clothing. When they leave, there is little food left for anyone else.

Don't trust those beady little eyes.

TROUBLE IN 1875

The people of North America found out how disastrous locusts could be in 1875. The skies went dark with swarms made up of trillions of locusts. The swarms looked like huge clouds, which would glitter as the light caught the locusts' wings. One writer described the feeling of the insects getting inside her clothes and being squished under her feet. The writer said that you "could hear the millions of jaws biting and chewing" as the locusts ate all the crops and food. The insects would beat their wings on the houses and windows as people hid inside. Sometimes they even got in, and could be found in people's beds!

One swarm was 177 kilometres wide.

SQUELCH!

Sometimes the locusts would gather on the warm, sun-baked train tracks to sleep. The trains would crush them as they went past. There were so many locusts that the oil from their squished bodies stopped the trains by making the wheels wet and useless.

The farmers tried to fight the locusts with fire and guns. However, there were far too many of the creatures for this to work. Other farmers used 'hopperdozers'. These were big sheets of metal that were covered in sticky tar and pulled along by horses. It would collect locusts like a giant scoop. However, even this idea wasn't enough to get rid of the hungry insects.

The locusts even pooed in the water, turning it brown and making it undrinkable. Is anything safe from locusts? (The answer is no.)

HOPPERDOZER

Some people abandoned their homes and tried to escape the swarms. The government sent help and food to the people who needed it. Things got much better and then, years later, the locusts suddenly disappeared. Nobody is sure why this happened.

Some scientists think that the locusts' eggs were destroyed accidentally by farming. Well done, farmers!

Pompeii

In Italy, there is a city frozen in the past. It is called Pompeii. Nobody lives there because the city is in ruins – but the ruins are perfectly **PRESERVED**. Jewellery, furniture and statues from long ago can all be seen in Pompeii. You can also see **CASTS** of people moments before they died, thousands of years ago. But how? This is the story of Pompeii.

Not everything in Pompeii survived until modern times – looters and thieves from Roman times tunnelled through the ash-covered city to steal things.

Pompeii was covered with around three metres of ash and debris.

A VOLCANO WAKES UP

In A.D. 79, Pompeii was a busy Roman city. It was just another day when, suddenly, a giant nearby volcano called Mount Vesuvius erupted after being quiet for more than 1,000 years. A cloud of ash and smoke rose more than 32 kilometres into the air. Some people ran to nearby villages, while others stayed in the city, hiding in their homes. Ash and debris began to rain down from the eruption. Fiery rocks fell from above. Soon, roofs caved in and buildings collapsed. The city, and everyone and everything inside it, was smothered with a thick, ashy powder.

One writer at the time described "great tongues of fire" coming from the volcano. It must have looked like the end of the world as the sky went dark.

MOUNT VESUVIUS

The eruption lasted for more than 24 hours.

FINDING POMPEII

Any survivors were soon killed by the pyroclastic flow that followed the falling ash and rocks. The heat was unbearable. It would have been impossible to breathe in the burning air. The eruption also destroyed a town called Herculaneum, and lots of nearby villages. Up to 30,000 people died in the A.D. 79 Vesuvius eruption.

During the 18th century, archaeologists found the ancient city of Pompeii. The ash that covered the city stopped it from being worn away and destroyed. Statues were found that looked as if they had been carved a week ago. When the archaeologists explored the market place, they found jars that still had fruit inside. They found graffiti on the walls. The graffiti of Roman times was a lot like the graffiti of our times; one Roman had written "Gaius Pumidius Dipilus Was Here". They also found **CAVITIES** in the ash, where the people had once been. By filling in these cavities with plaster, perfect casts of the people of Pompeii were made.

The casts of the people show what they were doing when the eruption of Vesuvius happened.

The Aleppo Earthquake

THE CITADEL OF ALEPPO

Aleppo is a city in Syria, in the Middle East, which still stands today.

230,000 people died in the 1138 Aleppo earthquake, which makes it one of the deadliest earthquakes in recorded history.

In 1138, a giant earthquake shook the city of Aleppo. A lot of it was destroyed, including the area around it. The walls of the citadel collapsed during the earthquake, along with many buildings, crushing those within. The city was already in trouble because there was a war going on between **MUSLIMS** and **CRUSADERS** from Europe. However, the natural disaster made everything much, much worse. During the earthquake, **RAIDERS** attacked the citadel by slipping through the broken walls.

It wasn't just Aleppo that was affected. Nearby, a crusader citadel was completely flattened by the earthquake. A village close to Aleppo was also completely destroyed; according to people at the time, the ground in the middle of the village completely opened up and there was a wide split in the earth.

WHY DO EARTHQUAKES HAPPEN?

You might be wondering how a city like Aleppo can be so unlucky when it comes to earthquakes. It is all to do with tectonic plates. Tectonic plates are huge slabs of rock. Some of the plates are as big as continents and oceans. Tectonic plates are always moving around slowly. However, if the plates bump into each other, or grind along each other, this can cause rumbles and shakes. This is what an earthquake is.

The plates move between 0 and 100 millimetres per year.

Aleppo was built in a dangerous place – unfortunately, nobody knew this at the time because people didn't know much about tectonic plates. In this part of the world, the African tectonic plate meets the Arabian tectonic plate. The area where two plates crash into each other is called a fault line. Aleppo is built on a **NETWORK** of these fault lines, called the Dead Sea fault system. This means that earthquakes are likely to happen in this area of the Middle East, and sometimes they can be very powerful indeed.

The Dead Sea is a nearby sea. It gets its name because no fish or plants can survive in its salty waters.

The movement of tectonic plates is also what causes volcanoes to form and erupt.

The Laki Eruption

Laki is a **SYSTEM** of volcanoes in Iceland. In 1783, one of the biggest eruptions in recent history took place. However, this eruption wasn't like others – instead of one big bang, Laki spewed lava and burped gas for eight months.

Pardon you, Laki.

A huge amount of gas and fire flooded out of Laki. Fountains of lava were spat into the air, and some of the plumes reached 15 kilometres high. Most of the lava was released in the first five months. A lot of sulphur also came out of the system of volcanoes. All this sulphur mixed with the rain to create acid rain – this is a harmful rain that destroys plants and harms people and animals. Laki's acid rain was so strong that it could burn holes in the leaves of trees, and cause damage to people's skin if they were caught in this dangerous downpour.

TREES DESTROYED BY ACID RAIN

Some of Laki's lava fountains were 800 to 1,400 metres tall.

The volcano released a type of **CHEMICAL** called fluorine, which seeped into the grass in Iceland. This was bad news for grazing animals, which eat grass. Over half of the animals, such as sheep and cows, died in Iceland because of all the fluorine. Crops were also destroyed, and in the end 10,000 Icelandic people were dead from hunger and disease. This was one-fifth of the whole population.

It wasn't just Iceland that was affected. The whole of the **NORTHERN HEMISPHERE** was covered in Laki's sulphur cloud. This meant the Northern Hemisphere had an extremely cold winter because of all the sulphur in the air. The Laki eruption proves that even a small island can have a big effect.

All over Europe, farmers began to mysteriously die as the toxic cloud spread, and nobody knew why.

Mystery Solved?

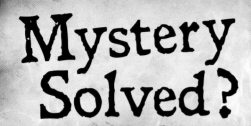

Did you find any disasters that matched our skeleton, here in the museum? If you said the eruption of Mount Tambora, well done! The powdery covering could be the ash and debris which covered everyone and everything. Mount Tambora is also in Indonesia, and erupted hundreds of years ago.

Perhaps this person was alive a few hundred years ago. They might have been a farmer who was using the rich soil around the volcano to produce huge crops! They might not even have known they were living next to a volcano all of their life would have gone dark and the lava would have started flowing. There would be a huge explosion and, before they knew it, they were covered in ash. If it was true, this is just one of the many stories that survive through time and history

Glossary

ASH a powdery material left behind after something is burnt

CASTS objects created by pouring a liquid in a mould and waiting for it to harden

CAVITIES empty spaces in solid objects

CHEMICAL a substance that materials are made from

CHRISTIANS people who believe in the religion of Christianity

CONTINENTS very large areas of land, that are made up of many countries, such as Africa and Europe

CROPS plants that are grown on a large scale because they are useful, usually as food

CRUSADERS people who fought in religious wars between 1096 and 1291 called the Crusades

CURRENT a steady flow of water in one direction

DEBRIS the remains of anything that has been broken down or destroyed

EVOLVED gradually developed and adapted to an environment over a long time

GASES air-like substances that expand freely to fill any space available

LIVERY HALLS buildings used by people in charge of certain groups of workers in London

MUSLIMS people who follow the religion of Islam

NETWORK a system of connected people or things

NOBLEMEN people who are part of the highest social class

NON-AVIAN not relating to birds

NORTHERN HEMISPHERE the half of the Earth that is north of the Equator

PARTICLES extremely small pieces of a substance

PERIOD a length of time

PLUME a long cloud

PRESERVED maintained in its original or current state

RAIDERS people who invade to attack and steal

RELIGIOUS relating to or believing in a religion

REMAINS parts that have been left behind; usually referring to a dead body

RESOURCES supplies of money, materials or people

SCIENTISTS people who study and know a lot about science

SPECIES a group of very similar animals or plants that are capable of producing young together

SUCCESSFUL when someone or something has done well

SYSTEM a series of things that are interconnected and perform a function

TECHNOLOGY machines or devices that are made using scientific knowledge

Index